REG SANER

SO THIS IS THE MAP

Random House New York

"April Campsite" and "Then Be Desert Air" first appeared in *Aloe;* "Interstate"
first appeared in *The American Poetry Review;* "Moon" first appeared in *The
Atlantic Monthly;* "And So We Climb Higher," "Scene for an Early October to
Come," and "Knowing Me Well" first appeared in *Aspen Anthology;* "August
Evening at Crater Lake" and "Rain" first appeared in *Back Door;* "Letter" first
appeared in *The Chowder Review;* "Leaving These Woods to the Hunters" and
"Ground Blizzard, Interstate 70" first appeared in *Colorado Quarterly;* "Swimmers"
first appeared in *Crazy Horse;* "On a Photograph of *Piazza del Duomo*" first
appeared in *Descant;* "Where I Come From" and "Prayer to St. Francis Among
Others" first appeared in *Epoch;* "Talking Back: A Dream," "Homing," and "A
Blue Glass Jar" first appeared in *Field 15;* "Orchestra" first appeared in *The
Georgia Review;* "What'll You Take" first appeared in *Graham House Review;*
"The Day the Air Was on Fire," "*Clarissima Lumina Mundi:* Visiting New York,"
and "Let's Say You Are This Page" first appeared in *The Iowa Review;* "Bonfires"
first appeared in *Ironwood 11;* "Milkweed" first appeared in *Mississippi Review;*
"From Chief Joseph I Turn the Page" first appeared in *New Letters;* "This Could
Have Been the Place" first appeared in *The North American Review* (Copyright
© 1976 by the University of Iowa); "Denver Planetarium: 'The Archive Project',"
"Anasazi at Mesa Verde," and "Lately I've Seen Myself" first appeared in
Northwest Review; "Clear Night, Small Fire, No Wind," "To Go No Farther"
(under the title "Stitchwork"), and "Mountain of the Holy Cross: San Juan
Range" first appeared in *Poetry;* "Congregation, Tableau" and "Packing In" first
appeared in *Poetry Now;* "Watching the Wet Birds Fly Through Cold Rain"
first appeared in *Prairie Schooner* (Copyright by University of Nebraska Press);
"Ploughing the Dark" and "Blue Sparrow Caper" first appeared in *The Salt Cedar;*
"Return to Tundra At Bighorn Flats" first appeared in *Three Rivers Poetry
Journal* (copyright © 1977 by Three Rivers Press).

Library of Congress Cataloging in Publication Data
Saner, Reg.
So this is the map.
I. Title.

PS3569.A5254S6   811'.54   80-6016
ISBN 0-394-51668-0
ISBN 0-394-74821-2 (pbk.)

For "Kate"
who gave me
my mother tongue

Obéissez à vos porcs qui existent. Je me soumets à mes dieux qui n'existent pas.

Nous restons gens d'inclémence.

René Char, "Contrevenir"

The author wishes to thank the University of Colorado Council on Research and Creative Work, and the National Endowment for the Arts, whose creative writing fellowship made possible much of the work in this book.

The National Poetry Series was established in 1978 to publish five collections of poetry annually through five participating publishers. The manuscripts are selected by five poets of national reputation. Publication is funded by James A. Michener, Edward J. Piszek, The Ford Foundation, The Witter Bynner Foundation, and the five publishers—Doubleday, E. P. Dutton, Harper & Row, Random House, and Holt, Rinehart & Winston.

The National Poetry Series, 1981

George Barlow, *Gumbo* (Selected by Ishmael Reed)
Larry Levis, *The Dollmaker's Ghost* (Selected by Stanley Kunitz)
Robert Peterson, *Leaving Taos* (Selected by Carolyn Kizer)
Michael Ryan, *In Winter* (Selected by Louise Glück)
Reg Saner, *So This Is the Map* (Selected by Derek Walcott)

CONTENTS

PART I

THE SIMPLE SIZE OF ALL WE BELONG TO

THE DAY THE AIR WAS ON FIRE
for Ron Billingsley

All afternoon neither of us said
"This air's on fire," though both felt it
and felt in sunlight like that, death
was impossible, or if possible, overrated,
even trivial. The sky kept showing off
in all colors, each of them blue
and we trekked that enormous plateau
whose tundra darkened or flared in one broad
autumnal crackle of burnt orange, then gold,
drifting under islands of cumulus
as if somebody'd laid out the pelt
from a sunset. Toward the nearest of two
schist cairns studding the highest stretches
we knelt and touched late gentian corollas,
still half bud. "How long till first snow?"
Days, not weeks. But with outcrops insisting
the last word should be rocks, then flaking
and falling away from that, we noticed
how each tuft put them to use
improvising soil from palmfuls of grit,
saying "If not this season, the next—
perhaps the one after," and coming on
very small, coming on uphill,
against everything.

MOON

Moon on the floating boredom of rowboats
at Spirit Lake, Iowa, on flanks of somnambulist Guernseys
drifting the feedlots
and on the great burial mound outside Kahokia

Moon on blue workshirts fingered by clotheslines,
on spin burnished into the sawmill's spare blade,
the crow's eye dismantled by ants,
the insomniac's watchband

Moon on chips in the bulldozer's gearshift knob,
on the black snake pausing at wheel ruts
and on the breathless steel mirror
nailed to the bathhouse door

Moon on Arizona butte-tops, their secret veins
of tourmaline, on cattle-guards marking access roads,
on breaks in the river, the island's fat leaves
and on the otter's nose, surfacing

Moon on rooftop antennae, the nightwatchman's key chain
and handcuffs, on the Art Institute's corridor wall
with 3 oils by Yves Tanguy

Moon on Ozark coon dogs and the pair
of teenage brothers who follow, on aluminum crumples
tossed aside near the mouth of the cave
and on ash flaking over the campfire

Moon on nightcrawlers fattening golf greens,
on the air's lathery riffles through cornfields,
on the widower's cigarette papers
and on the virgin lifeguard's legs, opening

Moon on cable-car rails flowing up Telegraph Hill,
on the photographer's trip-wire baited
for owls, and on plastic tubing of lawn chairs
whose arms harvest dandelion fuzz

Moon on rake tines, the door-knocker's dolphin,
the planter's ceramic glaze leaking fern, and on the white
white waitress barefooting it home from the bus stop
humming, dangling her sandals.

ON A PHOTOGRAPH OF
PIAZZA DEL DUOMO

This granite sarcophagus corniced with egg-
and-dart work spoke Roman, and if the figure
fronting his scallop-shell niche
was equestrian class
that sag on his head is a helmet
lifted for discourse.

Of his skin
one patch between collarbone and neck
remains smooth, whereas she has rained
to a chess pawn—her features,
like his, so overexposed
to water's way with limestone
there are none.

Despite their loss
of detail I congratulate both on happiness
and long life. Politely they observe
what a lovely morning it is
in the *Piazza del Duomo*
and that the translucent wing tips on pigeons
are right in applauding a sunlight
we'll never take with us. But already
a penitent carved
of gilt wood
and immortal portals densely populated
in bronze have remarked as much—
as who hasn't?

Because it's a speaking world. A world
where voices coming farthest to say so

come closest, and a place where no former holes
in this atmosphere
can be strangers, including this pair
of married stones taking me
for one of them, telling me how
the dead would be dead
right now, if they were not guests
in so many houses.

ANASAZI AT MESA VERDE
for Anne

I

Villages not half as wide
as a voice, their masonry boxes, tucked
under a tidal wave
of cliff. Bright sun, a surf
of oak. From one jar
pot-hunters' dynamite couldn't reach,
a dog-hair sash so tightly weft in grays
and umbers, its tassel ends
so fresh I can't believe
Dante died holding on to its other end
just as this urn of Anasazi corn
went underground. High at the back
on rock, "R. Wetherill"
in candle soot.

II

Even these fieldstone rooms
and towers, Florentine for color.
Were cities a hard birth?
Furrows begun with Abel, walls
with Cain—those two permanent lobes
of the mind. When its climate
is raids we huddle these rifts
while overhead as Menelaos, Hannibal,
Sigurd, Manfred, Guido Selvaggio
and other Apaches, we harvest
ourselves by spear. At night
the smell is Anglo-Saxon farms
gone smoke. When only the land is left
we follow spring up the ladders

where war has taught a burnt earth
making fire fit to eat.
The land is enough.

III

Around the smashed lip
a "spirit line" circling by yucca tip;
the little black-and-white motif
of deer. Shard upon shard
repeating each simple animal
as the river our steps must take.
From adobe layers we resume
wet palm prints tamped between courses
of stone. These kiva walls are round
as eggs, not tombs. Over roof clay
packed till it drums
they hatch us to leaping
and dancing, painting and making,
those ancient colonizations of light
by blood. How the shamans felt it,
and Thales, and Dante: pouring our village
of souls like a fistful of dust
into this perfectly usual sunset
and filling the air with gods.

IV

Come down into cliffs we wade
amongst lives where even sleepers
are workers. The squared lintels here,
that lion gate at Mycenae, still composing
our part in what the wind plays
as it follows this canyon's strange
bodies of space, its evening mazes
of heat traversed by the arrow and swerve
of hawks. With monoliths riffling

their shadows through pollen yellows,
ochres, slabs of hackberry blue,
oxides and rust, our rhythm becomes
obsidian scrapers, this weaving
of yucca, this fat grind of corn
mealed under the stone.
Our rain is bean poles and tendrils
and squash, "Green Table"
our land that goes on
passing through war and all things
giving itself away to keep on giving,
our singing, our hands, our stream.

AUGUST EVENING AT CRATER LAKE

Like a man in the midst of himself,
the map's blue lake going dark
within circles that brighten, widening
from the mouths of trout.
One huge surround of inhabited stone—
and green pine rotting ochre ledges
whose colors dazzle slowly
apart, weave a while in place,
then heal.
On the opposite shore a camper
works up a sweat under fading sky
flashed off an ax-blade. Each downward arc
hits the windfallen trunk as the start
of a silence taking a full
second to break.
No other sound but that . . .
and the flush of high snow, its dark streaks
harvesting cliffs old and roughly angular
as thunder.

A valley that ends
under this dim flitter of wings—
its single bat, then another, drawing twilight
in closer around the lake. And as if
to be taken personally, the first
half dozen stars over water
where even the great crags dream.
How many times will this happen
without me? Here in the simple size
of all we belong to, I sit very still,
the separate steps of a small breath
passing into strange hands.

PACKING IN

Your first surprise, leaving so much
of the stuff behind. Through hackled timbers
windfallen, meadow bogs sucking at bootheels,

across streambed whose pebbles flash
like old coins, along trail growing more
and more haggard, you lean upgrade toward

the pass as your forehead's sweating falls clear,
biting a dust that believes your body is crying—
except that the pain feels good, as if finally

getting you somewhere, maybe into the second
surprise, that nothing you'll need on the way
was ever too heavy to carry.

CONGREGATION, TABLEAU

Centered in the deepest hardnesses,
those we call boulders, a sort of Black Mass
goes on over rudiments of an altar
or near one.

The rocks themselves dimly apprehend that this scene
lodged within them is wrong. Not that there's any priest, or light
like the burning of sulphur
in darkness—though there is
something like that.

The deeper the boulder the more plausible, even innocent
its disguises.

Which is why all but the stones
are convinced of not feeling considerable numbers
inside; a congregation,
a vast tableau
in which no one stirs.

CLEAR NIGHT, SMALL FIRE, NO WIND

A lot of boulders lying around
giving off locked fires, but what for?
Warming ourselves at the memories of igneous lobes?
My thumbnail opens the parachute
on a first match that flares,
then settles and holds.

No wind at all.

Which surprises, here where slipstreams
of krummholz and knee-high fir
speed in place, formed to those winds
whose drifts they winter in
and live by. As the fire takes
I feed in crackles of twig, their gray sheen
dry and silvery, almost, as the early moon
nearly at full. Looking around I find
without my help it has already climbed
well above Sawtooth. Upper ledges of cirque
slowly forgetting the color of sunset, I imagine
myself back at Buchanan Pass, watching range
beyond range, each wave of peaks
bluer than the last, breaking
into the dusk like surf.

Then high country chill sets in
and the strongest stars burn daylight away
for the rest, till the sky's
that deeply intricate crown
fitting no one.

And my fire's a handwarmer, sinking toward
the beat and stutter of coals. The bottom star
of the Dipper nears ridgeline, diffracting
through gorse. Then the earth
turns it out. Despite all my trekking
plateaus, playing "if" on traverses, isn't this
what I'm here for? To sit warming myself
at the center of things that in an hour or so
will fall asleep in my outline. Staring
into dark forms that have taken eons
without me, yet resting content
with whatever it is that I come to.

A nothingness, breathing.
A moment, amazed at its size.

PART II

FROM CHIEF JOSEPH
I TURN THE PAGE

FROM CHIEF JOSEPH
I TURN THE PAGE

From Chief Joseph I turn the page
into a platoon of the 7th Cav., 1890
and Progress still driven by horse.
These were the men at Wounded Knee. A trooper
prone and aiming into the lens says down
this barrel I'm studying early stages
of Interstate 80. Another's vain, shows
the strongest side of his head and a brow
gone pale from hats. At 12 he handled
one of those 6-horse gang-plows Chicago invented
for digesting Nebraska; from the root cellar
hefted 100-lb. sacks. At 16 he left.

The trooper not here is underground
still drunk, an arrowhead pinned to a bone.
In the 3rd row, kneeling, one of the Trimble boys
from home. When he and Nile fell out over a wife
he didn't just stomp his brother's face,
he set a roweled heel on the nose and lips,
then stood, and spun. Here with the grass
still flat it's winter or early spring.
A few wear bear paws for mitts. Not one uniform
looks spruce. Which is the officer—that ramrod
fading out of print on the left?
His cousin's still mayor of Cairo Illinois
for the next 100 years. When I was a kid
they caught the dentist treating Blacks
hog-tied him into his chair, doused kerosene,
and lit the match. But which of them knows
a few buffalo words in Sioux or Cheyenne?

Jaw muscles grown pulling back on reins.
Their trigger fingers drove the Golden Spike.
Our worst diseases come disguised
as cures. Now that the West is won
these men are wrong. Where are they standing?
The land my house is on? I see old-time
brass buttons, tunics, hammerlock carbines
saying I could not have been there,
and these faces, saying I am.

INTERSTATE

For the one trip of the year
my speedometer readout is cash
shooting feedlots past
where comatose Angus knead muck
rich as their coats, slobbering troughs,
lowing like Israel in Egypt, bearing
that double-golden yoke
of McDonald's. I flip off
pulled up by a Texaco pump,
its hose sucking fresh credit
out of my tank.

Looking around I sense it again.
This side of the road is weird.
A station's red sofa, weathered pale
with old men, their neckskin in flaps,
faces half-mooned by controls
on the Pepsi machine. They watch.
Near Rexall Drugs, the grainsack wives—
lifers welded inside gravel-bitten trucks,
waiting for men who pretend
at gazing deep into windows
of parking meters, their talk
run thin as winter creeks.

Strangers go through as loud riffles
of dust eating this road on money.
It scares. Down the street,
that chalk barn where Christ
is nailed to one wall.
These black coveralls bending up
from under my hood. "Water pump's shot,

block cracked." Staring.
Shifting his grease rag from fist
to fist. Till I admit my check's
no good? As if he knew. And they.
As if for years.
Have known it never was.

WHERE I COME FROM

Where I come from the bright ones
left the farm. What this picnic snap
doesn't show is Uncle Cyril
who wanted to write for the slicks
selling Porta-Pools, the *Americana*, cable TV.
And what Grandad Rexroat can't see here
is how a man could lose
even this land·we're standing on.
Uncle Frank's first, Aunt Maude, hates
his farming so much she pours dishwater
into his lap before taking off. Her big idea
is L. A. Aunt Minta writes she's there yet,
visiting Helen Frances up in Palm Springs
while Frank switches wives like two-tone shoes.
Mail from Uncle Lee in Fort Wayne plugs thrift,
the G. O. P., and Kroger stores
because he owns stock. In Omaha
the feed-cattle Grandad buys to come back
can't quite believe in his luck, so he develops
a window-screen/storm-window route,
raking leaves off the rich end of town.
Each birthday card has heft, its 50-cent piece
Scotch-taped, fire-new from the mint.
I answer by pencil, each word fat,
but never answer enough. From Toledo
Uncle Cyril considers retiring early on fiction
he's still planning to write. This picnic's
our last where Grandmother Rexroat
has full use of both hands. RM lolls
in sandals and curls on that wide
hammock of staves. The elms go deep.
The new porch's paint looks fresh

to the touch. I can see that towheaded
dwarf they're aiming into the lens
hasn't a clue how far
he's squinting from there,
with somewhere a city for each of us.

GROUND BLIZZARD, INTERSTATE 70

A starved light, lavishing pain
and inch-high torrents of satellite weather
sucking across like cirrus. My brakes
are second and first. From gust
to gust our Ford hood gets lost.

We crawl it back. A blue seed flashes,
develops its plough underneath—safe
but slow as a barn door.
Anne presses her lips. She knows
they've trained me to pass.
The Interstate Escadrille—each hangar
coded Food/Service/Gas. Fellow aces
stoned on mileage, chocolated
hot water, staring 3 feet ahead
sipping nothing but road.
How our neck tendons ache!

Lungs filling with glass, we shuffle
dimpled ice hand over hand
into our crusted 4-door. The snow tires
whine like slow learners trying too hard,
taxiing us up into air getting worse.
To ease right or left my insides
clench, but ditched machines I still
decal to the fuselage. Whiffling
past this yellow Merc our full
fat 50 carries nearly too far.
Out of its slow parallel swerve
my grin cringes back.

Mile after mile our 2 sons doze
in the mirror, Dacron cocoons
not even scared, their windows
a breath of white crows.

LETTER
after a phrase by **Quasimodo**

Ponds and ditches in a moss lather.
That team of Percherons nickering beyond
the barn. From new cocklebur clusters
you press doll's chairs, a rug. For babies,
clay roots tugged loose near the bank
and now this 747 oozing up,
docking at Concourse B.
With a window seat confirmed I climb
into the attic on East State, finger antique
high school texts—your Shakespeare cued
for Portia; Stevenson, Scott; Caesar's *Wars*;
your Virgil pale in blue buckram,
its penciled scansion running
50 years back. What kept by heart
surprised us both. The table's oilcloth
glares and our stovefront's enamel clock
stays stuck because I'm handling
eram eras erat like brick
years short of the poem.

How long, *mater dulcissima*, can your hobby
be these annual travels and tears
you know I won't have? Germless acres
of chrome shuffling family trees by ramp
and red carpet freight, bringing my ritual
jokes to that on-flight Scotch
of your choice. Fast cloud up there
for staring leagues down,
into the tears in things. Below,
an underworld pallor our winter hills
can't shake—like this distance

we keep putting off. "Maybe next summer.
We'll see." And nod, as if. Each flight
your father tools home to the farm's
barrel-stave hammock, its geysering lilacs
and elms, herding the first Model A.

Time after time these strange
machines carrying us nearer the edge
of sound. Is it now I press 2 obols
into your palm? "Not yet, not yet,
we've lots of these glimpses left"—
each one closer, farther. Aboard you wave
across baggage crews finishing up
under gold swashes streaming
a 3-story rudder; but already
I'm slipping back through vinyl tunnels
to the upper-lot deck, with 40 miles
of turnpike to say, "*dulcissima,
mea dulcissima mater.*"

DOC HOLLIDAY'S GRAVE

"How many men did he kill, really?"
Far below us the great white ox of Colorado sun
muscles valleys, and a stream bossing roads around
into and out of Glenwood Springs
whose voluptuous prospect of green, ore-bearing hills
seems nudes, oiling whorehouse bars. "How many
would we say's enough?" Because "too many" feels **good**
we climb leisurely on toward the morning's
mountainside grave where a Byronic dentist
from Valdosta, Georgia, followed T.B. and whiskey
to a pair of rag lungs. In Tombstone
or Dodge wasn't it true? That at the lightest wrong
word our right hand was a blur
long since broken out into sage, juniper,
rabbit-brush, yellow wallflower, and myth we enter
through movies where only the horses
are sane: the Ophir Saloon, where our cock
pumps through clouds of black powder
its thunder into another man's chest.
John Henry Holliday, D. D. S.,
who dealt faro and knew the value of flash.
His .45 nickel-plated; his gravestone incised
with aces spreading like a lover's bouquet,
wooing suckers to step outside
the law and draw first. And beautiful how many
at the O. K. Corral: where we stand
till our overcoat sleeve grows a sawed-off shotgun
ploughing Tom McLowry's liver and groin
like Cain's wet dream, a wealth of it spilling
all the way here, right at our feet.

LEAVING THESE WOODS
TO THE HUNTERS

The carcass hangs by a grease rope,
head and legs hacked off,
but still big as a small elk.
Under sumac clumps a skirmish
of arctic jays redden breast plumage
nagging tufts from hide
stuck to one hoof.

The earth turns slowly as fog.

This son of a bitch has come prepared—
long-bladed kitchen knife, whetstone, steel!
He never heard of weight.
Lightly he strops at the pelt
and its meat side, a damp pearlescent gray,
falls of its own heft.
Through naked aspen
the October sun is a yolk.

Downstream kneeling to drink
I take in the smack of salt.
Deer's blood?
My pack harness creaks
as wiping my chin I glimpse a face
that shines like an otter's neck,
its sleek light rippling
distortedly in place. Poor creature,
and merciful liar.

Yet I'll slog downtrail
leaving these woods to the hunters,
having never myself
killed anything
more beautiful than a man.

PART III

THE INWARDNESS
OF FIRE

DENVER PLANETARIUM: "THE ARCHIVE PROJECT"

I

This teacup hemisphere's where we go in
for the science of reach, its 2 lobes
intricate, mechanical, the split
head of a fly. From them we pour
the wild interior as solar winds
on the face, and stars coming out
of the ceiling. If we gasp at that
it's because seeds
are concentrates. Leverage
of a few lenses and bulbs, their burst
of milkweed turning the earth.

II

Talking the universe into ourselves
we tilt back in seats like a nap
that's immense. Nebular
butterflies underwater. Now Cassiopeia?
The Pleiades cluster? Among vanishing points
thicker than static we're roots of a cave
sleepwalking through snow. Hidden speakers
insist on plot: "12 intragalactic
elect have pooled data banks to explore
our galaxy's central monstrous
black hole," its enormous affluence
a holocaust of force. Around the rim,
projectors, 79, zapping readout like flak.

III

In all that char and flare, "Seeking
higher intelligences than their own."

A blue binary star. Our daily bread,
the self as loot buried elsewhere—
and speakers laying it on with slides
whose giant's that red bloat
eaten by the usual white dwarf,
its gallows of light, strange
as a grandmother's night-blooming cereus.

IV

NASA decals. Our space ship
a breakthrough riding gravity waves
for fuel. Archived aboard, all that 12
planets could learn—enough to admit
"No return is planned."
But what's *out* there? A wealth
of death? Window to Universe B?
No help from the script,
a shill, sci-fi hints leaving us
ravenous for fact. Here the deepest light
is paint, a clever chirr of gears
faking us out of the cave
on 2 flints and a language that says
what Copernicus saw we knew at the door
and know we're travelling it still;
this simple inwardness of fire, going out
where these stars join,
in where our house has its roof.

NIGHT EVENT

My footprints lock. A shadow
coming slowly onstage; our bodies and brains
quietly eating this bright circle
of flesh. Scanning the vague curve
its terminator makes I marvel
at flat-earth ancients missing clues
written broadly as that.
Yet it goes deep. The eye
in its savage state.

And things go on. Beyond Dakota Ridge
our deer sleep it out under trees.
I feel the almond iris of the coyote
blur. Under tumbleweed, a small lizard
hugging his shale chip, whetting his tongue.
Penumbral orange, giving way
like heat loss. A neon bone
riding further into the umbral dark
ruddied by light rays warped
through our breath.

Along the mesa, infrared snakes
wrinkling nearer to field mice; radar bats
flying out of the ground. The rummage
of porcupine, nevertheless. And sleepers
turning their backs on this dream.

At full eclipse we touch
its actual rondure and heft, feel in our sky
this stone enormous as an emptied room
rolling through every day of our lives.
The oldest memory, hanging huge

and weightless and still—telling how little
we live in this world, or any other,
at what unfathomable speeds.
And under us all, the sun
burning like rain.

CLARISSIMA LUMINA MUNDI: VISITING NEW YORK

From a great way off through roar and doze,
waking to twilight by jet, all dinosaurs gone,
the kerosene storm on our tail
straining us down
into these landscapes of the made, down
to be the man in waders, vacuuming green concrete
under the corporate building's lagoon,
the man with the dollar bill in his mouth,
the man who rams his fantasy .38
into the throat of each dog, and pulls.

At the Whitney's exhibit, 2 pick-up trucks—
a white one blued by felt-tip with hatchure marks
taking weeks, whereas the black truck
is pencilled all over in scrollwork fine
as Da Vinci's silverpoint grotesques
or that queer vegetation
on money and stocks. A mini-career right there.
As to say: "We take such pains," and
"The Sistine is equally blank."

An F train oils the platform's subway atmosphere,
shooting carloads of jobs across my face
by express. Through their blur I stare
into somewhere else, the way, at a certain speed
passing cracks in a backyard fence,
cedar slabs become a transparence.
Then out again, into the dusk air, glimpsing
through light rain in the Village
an Indian, hurrying, sheltering his guitar.

MILKWEED

Acres to pick from.
This green and celery stem I snap
oozes glue at its heel-ends while both lungs inflate
for a blow
burring my lips till they tickle.

A few parachutes leak at once to earth, others float, riding
thin warps in the air like veins.

The game's to try again and again
how many hundred yards the furthest breath carries,
watching its endlessly invisible difference
sown in the field.

PLOUGHING THE DARK
for Les Brill

Isn't it enough that a forest stands
at the edge of a man being eaten
by a lit cigarette? His face disappears,
reappears. His eyes have travelled here
from bouillon. A squirrel's shadow streams
down an oak, a few frogs creak like chairs.
One barleycorn grit—on the road
since when?—strikes air like a match,
its meteor ploughing the dark, fading
on retinal nerve. He has seen a boulder-size
hunk, come to earth for an Arizona blacksmith
to anvil away on for years, malleable
as nail metal. You could stipulate burial,
he supposes, clenching bits of it
in your right hand. Perhaps shoe a horse.
As if there were any other way.

In the Smithsonian, an Egyptian crisp
as winter sycamore leaf before it floats off
is lying alone in his glass case, a prim card
listing stomach contents recovered—some granules,
apparently wheat, having swum like Jonah
through the painted dreaming of tomb walls
onto this bowl.

Once a horticulturalist from Japan
showed him slides of a lotus recollecting itself
from seed 1,800 years old, waiting
in certain layerings of Honshu peat
for an audience. As if out of night sky
the petals open, perfectly formed.

41

Imponderable tonnages all around, hurtling,
burning. He lights a fresh cigarette,
then returns his look to gardening the stars.
Natal physics, brilliancies his eye
can never take in, except finally.
What percent has consciousness? His estimate
trudges miles, carrying a decimal point
to its blind address. 10 to the 18th?
Even less? Meanwhile the city's houses
are tired. In some of them, hovering
cantaloupe rind by the sink are fruit flies
whose forelegs end in nerve distinguishing
5 different sugars. But the houses
are tired, the houses are weary,
and the people are bored.

THE DAWN COLLECTOR

And the southern sky's faintest stars slip away, tambourines
shaken just out of earshot.

Do we feel dawn "auspicious" the way we know it's a planet,
because people have said so? Hopeful as the habits of birds
each twist, neural meteor
through the brain.

The reservoir, a dilute wash of madder, heartens
beyond the power plant's triple stacks. 3 small doe,
lovable mouth-slaves, flicker nostrils
toward our freshly bedded tomato sets
till my glare sidles them off—rejoining a buck
also young, in velvet. Their hoof-toc xylophones,
crossing asphalt.

Along Yucca Drive the deer and the sky
are the only ones stirring.

Like an elderly relative making sheer earliness virtue
I mix insomnia with the east, collecting 365 daybreaks
by Pentax, a coloring book of pink Continentals.
Yet no matter how numb I am, or how absent
dawn's nimbus
of melon rind tints in transition
always flutters the ghost in my machine.

Light's magnetic fields?

Something like that,
every time this Colorado plain brightens, tightens
to an edge, a hot copper wire

juiced toward the melting point of a day
that never happened before, verging
on now.

Within an arc of incandescent air
that called my mother's mother from hers
time hits the rim
as if blood, sizzling apart in my iris
like a burst sac-of-waters.

Out of the gone hands
holding my breath
the sun rises
primevally raw—kindling, fusing, granulating
whatever's in range so freely it doesn't matter
annihilation centers the sacred
where all illumination
implodes. This is the radiance
nothing survives, sidereal mirage flashing me
to the head of a past where the dark catches fire,
where the fire became what I am.

TRAIL

Footprints through snow, blue,
very thin. Set in each heel, melting,
a glacial stone smooth as the meter
of an old song. Our emerald hide flares,
sequins like aspen, but for a time
we'll rest content just whetting
a long coral tongue
on that lovely old bone the moon,
then begin to reflect: advance, meaning flight.
Past wind-torn gobbets of bristlecone pine
white and stringy as chicken meat,
past trail pebbles that want to be teeth.
Meanwhile that slow, venerable membrane
the sky—how she creaks! And dark green sorrowing
of boughs. Into the lunar silences we send
examples of ourselves. But now
the syllables tire of crippling along,
the brain malingers, fixes dimly
on basalt, still leading
the slowest of lives. Flake
after flake, the ice petals us open.
Words scale away and clatter
into trash couloirs, those chittery
encyclopedias of tears again weighed down
into underground currents pressed flat.
Their mica outcrops gather a light
that glitters and waits, thin
and patient as wings.
As footprints.

A BLUE GLASS JAR

A sunset like a total word.
Minutes after, the west
quiet as a shadow whose barn
has swallowed doves.

Ripe cottonwood leaves
flashing the last of the clouds
and first stars, dim
as insect wings.

The ants, pushing our dust around.

In one of my lives, surely,
I'll remember a blue
glass jar
that swims as it walks, keeping
a half dozen fireflies
surrounded.

PART IV

HOMING

SWIMMERS

At night after the valley has filled,
after the town has quenched and gone under
swimmers ooze from bedroom windows, glide between houses,
follow streets with closed lids
feeling the turns through shut lashes.

Like the smoke of white limestone
fluent rifflings travel their nightclothes.

Regardless of age each swimmer cruises in search of his double
or hers. Those sinking
lower, a bit lower each night are the old
whose clenched eyes
purse up skins infiltrated by sand. Yet how easily
the younger ones flow, like breath
into the simplest words.

LATELY I'VE SEEN MYSELF

It's one of those mornings—
April sky, these clouds inviting us
out of ourselves, melting snow
revealing the missing grain
of the wind. Lately I've seen myself
as making a hole in the light
the light should have back,
seen each boulder as home.
From its yucca stalk,
winter-killed, a meadowlark
splits its bill to call. Staring
into my shadow, I listen.

LET'S SAY YOU ARE THIS PAGE

Listen, only the real is intolerable.
Last evening I sat holding a book of poems
in this fixed stampede of talus
at the beyond of a mountain so remote
we'll have to imagine. Ragged boulder field,
saying all the buffalo have come here to die.
From a surround of peaks, June snow works
invisibly loose beneath the surface
in low, irregular halts, gargles, sobs
leaking away like an underground sunset.
The west reddens, sinks past the edge
of invention, where it warms each hide.
No, that's imagined. But not these hidden
wrist-thick streams I could follow
till they flash like snowfields
against another man's seamless sky.
Let's say you are this page
by Gunnar Ekelöf, looking up into eyes
going dark beside a blue tent. Let's say
you're now seeing alpenglow on a face
dimming, becoming part of a vast magnificent
loneliness so real that being here
doesn't matter. Is there a single bird?
Surely there must be, somewhere.

AND SO WE CLIMB HIGHER

Up ledge-lines disheveled
then across, aiming
to enter ourselves as no longer
a force, nor even a presence.

Some outcrop, alpine plateau enriched
with no one at all.

Messes of tundra hummocked alone
for their half-million blooms every 6 bees,
or cirque whose one thought is voles
and ground squirrels
curdling by night as coyotes
report to the stars.

Surely up there.

Where glacial runoff tatters down
over shelf-rim, its vacant billows
gusting moss into clefts.

And so we climb higher,
always higher.

TALKING BACK: A DREAM

We always said we would.
10 in line. The basketball coach on my right
dribbles a poem made up of periods strung
like ticks in a clock. Another, a girl,
is saying "Good-by EKG."
All of us writing farewells to our deaths.
They flow onto the page, not bad not good.
After, they'll wire our skulls for twitch.
Nobody cancels a line.

Through rooms my going empties behind.
The first knob was always the last.
A .22 is small but the feel is final.
They mean it, they'll finish us off.
Headlong through the window's a choice
that doesn't occur. I imagine the splash.
Down the row of heads toward me, little bursts
of *coup de grâce*, like stapling reports.
This isn't deciding, it's force.

Their grove of legs around me, and talk.
A blip of lead in the brain. I lie
very still, at the focus
of nothing. Daylight, blue trees, and time
like snow. This hive of life, these cells.
Something's told them I'm close.
The mind's a child, using the edge
as a club. Hasn't the body
rights of its own? Poor thing,
I pity it. Talking back, trying to reason
through dream. And the hearse doors, opening
wide on each side, like wings.

WHAT'LL YOU TAKE?

This is where you'd hoped not to be
what you are. Never mind the *tristesse au jour*,
it's time to select. What'll you take?
Those cavernous elms you grew up under?
They'll always be seeds. Island of birds
in the creek? Or October slashes of cornstalk
where your ballcap cocked at a locomotive
sounding one long word, low and far off,
about evening in Russia.

You will take, of course, the sister
who always was there, and the sister who died.
Meanwhile, what have you meant to anyone?
How can you take 2 sons already becoming
plans of their own? Didn't you actually marry
the most beautiful woman you ever saw,
then refuse to believe it? Better take them
as all of your failures. Who else
could give them that kind of care?

You are going to take a 4th birthday
when your fingers were cake; and the pressure
your grandfather's hand left in a work glove.
And the first bird's nest you ever found,
its one egg like the blind end
of the candle. For dog-day afternoons,
your grandmother's iris, purple tongues
fagging out. A few red-tail hawks weaving high air
over Uncle Frank's wheat. For residual ancestors,
add your collection of blue stones
that still dream they are speaking.

Instance: a ponderous father on empty staircase
left over from the missing house, his footstep
every so often strumming the shadows.
What did your mother take? One or two smiles
of compressed sawdust painted as dolls' heads?
A horse, perhaps, nickering; that hasp
on the root-cellar doors. Night windmill
whose creak kept the watering trough full.
And what did your father take? Homemade wagon,
maybe the one pulled by pet goat
in the only photograph. A small high-button shoe,
cow horn hollowed for BBs. Who knows?
A mistrust of all he had chosen?

And who are you now, knowing, like everyone,
you're certain to make it? A head
only hard things have ever gone into. Skinful
of snapshots; his voice, his fingerprints.
Good. Like hostile brothers come together
in a sadness whose light has grown far slower
than wheat, you're content adding up to one more
of the way things are; having in common,
now, the missing feel of that shore
he too was standing on, and never reached.

RAIN

after Jorge Luis Borges

Guttural air that suddenly lifts
when rain sets in, falling carefully enough
to go on all night. Falling, or fell,
because this rain I hear is always one
coming down a great while back.
The trash lid pattering
like columns of newsprint blown
across scrollwork on green-and-white
garden chairs. Leaves and petals
among the shot zinnias flick,
or flickered—the ear recalling
an afternoon's bizarre wads and clots
whose color a grandmother names
once and for all
to be *rose*. Lost suburbs. Fingertips
cloyed, still, on burst persimmon, its rust sac
slumping wet gravel. Windows that warp,
thrash, dimple in gusts
like garden plants where the house drifts
toward another city.

Brittle with drought their stems yaw,
tossing in rain, taking heart.
An arbor of grapes that darken, streaming.
Vines climbing like smoke, above
a puddled *cortile*; this dinner hour
light that draws wire thin
at a tile edge, then breaks
into beads. And voice not quite
overheard of my father, returned
from a trip, not death.

HOMING

Tracking deep signals given off
by the pronoun *I*, my feet
chew into the valley by switchback.
Stone air, empty of birds. An arctic cony,
silvery forelegs combing out his rich
mustache of dwarf clover
for drying on rocks. At a bend
the prospect clears through aspen;
pale bodystocking bark, lucent swivels
of leaf. To show nervous cloud fuming
the divide's raw edge—and one huge
conifer valley swathing miles
toward Bierstadt moraine. Austere cirques
at its end, risen high, barren,
beyond. These solitudes we must lose
in order to enter them.

Not a single blue thread unravelling
a campfire. Last winter's faint roar.
Down again, following knuckled trail
past Cenozoic grimaces barely
stopped short of intelligence, but walking
amongst myselves, homing
on forested inscape. Their breath
at the tip of the ear: "Never.
No one. None."

Muskrat entrails, split. A swipe
of visceral glue over alpine flowers

57

yellower than forsythia. Meaning mountain cat
on the prod? Blossoming out into space
this magnificently still, I imagine
maybe nothing can leave; imagine a hand
all pelt and claw, grazing these 3-week
shadows of seeds. Fast shadow grazes my face,
its light plane a droning, final machine
growing distant as a wren's eye.
Then after. The start of a silence
so immeasurable I keep lounging pine straw
pacing it off; staying put,
just taking its length.

IV

The sun blurts up again, again—
spinning BB in a can. Chipmunks,
otter, marmots, creep toward me
from the underbrush hackles
of gray timber wolf logs
as if toward a stream: nosing around,
expecting I'll join. Stands
of Engelmann spruce rise, improvise,
and die. August stars turn in this wind
strumming a ribcage whose body
is learning to wear articulate moons
on its sleeve; and October frosts arrive,
surrounding filaments of each eyelash
like the velvet antennae
of deer. Nights, I dream small fires
shut up in stones, and sunsets
of navigable rock flying off as vast
cavernous birds
into the same bronze egg.

V

With lichen seeping across my forehead
mapping ignorant countries
that want to be leaves, I become visits
of transparent ants, their dew
nudging last flecks of cell
to climb out of roots, unfurl,
then rappel by umbilical cord
back into the earth. My stare,
little hammers of black light nagging
at passer-by planets to see themselves
as they are: revolutions
of slate replacing a name once bitten
by rainbows. And all desire, all despair—
these two skyline monoliths jutting the rim
of glacial cirque. A pair of monks who look on
sitting quietly together, reading
even humming, the one book.

PART V

TO GO FARTHER

BLUE-EYED HEAD WITHOUT BEARD

A severed head is flying on wingbeats of hair,

as if toward a word in its mouth, a distant sound, one
thumb-worn as beads. Most decrepit of syllables
yet the one that came furthest to find me.

"So where are we now?"

The mirror's war-games, reflecting ennui and animal waters.
"Is this me, really?" "Piss off!"

Abraham's knifeblade plunging
and the hand of the angel who stays him.

"But who are we really?" "A warm wind, an inquest."

Meaning here at the window habitually uttering prayers
of description? Or astride my horse of gray felt
galloping always in the opposite direction, encoding secrets,
publishing keys. Hiding my body everywhere
so no one can miss it.

I sit staring at a cliff. Moments ago a cloud knocked
and entered. Inside I hear screaming and darkness.
"What's going on in there?" "You are."

At the end of the sky hovers a distance nobody believes
ever made darkness impossible. "So what
does that leave you?" A scene-change.

A staircase forever in flight
whose crash occurs every other reflection.

This blue-eyed abyss
punished with wings.

TO GO FARTHER

A German shepherd with iron teeth
leaps straight for my eyes, which clench
and unclench, soaking into dim phosphorescences
from a wristwatch. 3:30.

Gathering round the crash's single
survivor, a wall's rectangular streetlight,
stacked books near the bed, wadded Levis,
missing glass knob from one drawer—
all stitch my face back together
as the dog's open-jawed lunge
melts like a snowman.

As usual I wander awhile to make sure
of the house, slipping into rooms,
looking down at my sons to guess
what they, too, might have been
if I hadn't raised them. These days
I say "different, not better," refusing
to set off along the edge of night waters,
cutting my throat on a seashore.

I'm through with all that. This time
a dog, not a corpse. Yet it's clear.
Wherever I am, I have to go farther.

ORCHESTRA
for Denny Fischer

The conductor's cocked twig turns out to be
mountain hike through the kettledrum's buttered thunder
and a flute
birdwatching our daydreams. Then tremolo
slurs the violin-section's left fingers in unison
like sand-lilies curled against wind.

Lull of bassoons, solo trumpet. And back to the bones
of this music we came for; since we came to hear structure
but find the female bassist pretty. Or pretty, considering.
And a strain colonizing us earlier as oboes
claims us again as trombones
flowing underground, swimming past ore lying in veins
of solar gold like smashed cars, delving geodes of mineral skies,
white tie and tails, durable evening gowns
giving lessons by day, not making much money.

But we've come to follow album notes. Except for this sadness
hearing dull uncles, aunts, neighbors, secondhand cousins
tell us all they had meant to say,
this sadness at finding we love them
in the faces of strangers, the fog wrists of cellos
turning us into little wells of deep space,
pouring us into and out of our lives
like all we had meant them to be
if only we had remembered.

PRAYER TO ST. FRANCIS
AMONG OTHERS

As against dark thoughts, St. Francis,
let me not forget where I am.
Defend me from that.
Defend me from it Li Po, Joe Gould, St. Paul
and Pythagoras and Buddha and Lili Tofler.

Let my eye fall lovingly, lovingly.
On the sow's bristle, the ladybug's carapace.
On the Milky Way's prodigal mountain creek
pouring fern seed, ploughshares, hollyhocks
and crocodiles,
and flamenco guitars and mice.
Let me not dwell on the .38's muzzle
as keyhole, or envy those stepping off
into gravity's easy answer
definitively met. Let me between the ginkgo tree
and the mayfly remember even a few
Chinese fishermen dipping nets
for bread into Honan's night river,
their small boat bobbing above enormous carp
wiser than taproots.

Winters when my daylight locks on North
let me go out into the clear nights
looking up. Let me look up voluptuously,
allowing no naked-eye constellation
to die of my ignorance. Let me consider
example: a life so poor you owned it all—
the arctic fox homing under the flattest sky,
the caterpillar husk, the jaguar's spots—
believing your numbered circles around the sun

made part of this world's rainbow prayer,
only dark when we are.

As against any whining of thin blood
let my words reflect this actual earth
wholeheartedly, heartily.
If not your faith in those hosannas
heard beyond the stars, lend me, St. Francis,
lend me your answerable verve.

APRIL CAMPSITE

Darkness to warm them, stub-ends
of thimbleberry twigs flicker and bud like sleep
traversed by a voyage.

In my down bag I dream bells under the earth
and a woman whose embroidered hem sashays with her calves
as she traipses pine straw through woods
gathering my bones.

"Wake up," she whispers
"I've washed last winter's mirrors like dishes."

True enough, though it's early.

In the northerly lake I can still see
cup-stars of the Big Dipper, and in its southerly twin
dawn's glance off the water. April's new moon
tossing the night on its horns.

THEN BE DESERT AIR

Through blood pillars whose buttes
loom terrain frightened by eons—till I wonder
what's worse: desert wind single-minded as nails
or hammer-and-blowtorch sun
on these high, lateral storms of ocean bed
made, unmade, re-made
where no leavings are final.

Then the miracle, nightfall.

With evening's earliest stars
distinctly distant as the best of my qualities
the half-moon, rising, turns withered, desolate things
into my favorite garden. For shadows, lunar animals
call softly to each other. At the base of dunes
smoother than mountains under sheets
moonlit yucca bristle
proudly as turkey cocks.

And the mind's blue prism relents,
no longer picking its way through bleeding tableaux.
My ambitions? My father's?

Forget them a while. Watch the sky's 3½ clouds
come to a standstill.
Let clear desert moon preside
over drinkable twilight of cedarwood
and barberry drift asking no questions.

Then be desert air.

The way this red iron of buttes
steps out of gravity
into dream. The way all motionless things
seem wise, taking me with them, at home being no one
I ever tried to become.

PART VI

THIS COULD HAVE BEEN THE PLACE

NEW SNOW

Because it has fallen all night
like some vague mother of dreams
unlocking us from ourselves,
I rise before dawn and go out—
under elms, black trunk, black branch,
each involved with its beautiful spook—
between power poles where the light
travels by rope, into the open field.
Below, our dark town draws its soft
stone breath. Along this slope,
boulders like curds, and clumped gorse
nodding heavy as cauliflower—
great empty-handed donors
grown in weightless air. A mile off
through last week's frozen ruts
a car crunches away, as over the boards
of an old bridge. Walking slowly
among weeds whose stalks
like forgetful birds
are still taking weather in
through delicate bones, I pause.
The low clouds pause with us.
Everything speechless.

WATCHING THE WET BIRDS FLY
THROUGH COLD RAIN

Since winter won't quit I move to the other side of my head
finding the window's same year of cold rain:
what to do what to do what to do
to no end, merely

wet flitters of birdwing. As if on rails
the droplets slide steel clothesline, touch, merge
and condense brightnesses out of overcast grayer than wire.
Things got started,
then what? The garden's pear blossoms rise
from black trunk, whitely as ice water, stuck.

And the massed alders darken, streaming.

Swamped in sodden grass
a bit of carrot-skin beak on a blackbird flicks
now this way now that. Otherwise, these bare

lateral rovings of briar
where I watch and I watch more droplets bead coldly,
slowly, till each one entirely encloses a thorn
in this life that won't burn, and a sky
unbudged, and a garden refusing to circle.
All afternoon without end

dusk, or almost,
and the wet birds fly through cold rain
singing, insisting.

RETURN TO TUNDRA AT BIGHORN FLATS

for Anne

4 years back, far from the lines of your hand,
this mountain was it. I hiked into dead rock
till stone spoke more deeply than anyone.

Stunned on packweight, blank sun, thinned oxygen,
I took talus piles for insane civilizations
drawing me in, out of the lines of your hand,

prophesying my name as ruin, till granite
held me at gunpoint and wind was a thug
with stone propositions deeper than anyone's.

Climbing to keep my misery pure I knocked
at odd cairns, bone eclipses spelling
dim wreckage into the lines of all hands.

But this is not where I am, with mountains
that emptied a house. That was then—petrified smoke
drawing me deeper, further than anyone,

into iron seams like mean blue mouths sewn shut.
How could blind rock go deeper than anyone?
The plan of its temple is wind. No slabs
spell my name. Only the lines of your hand.

BLUE SPARROW CAPER

He chins himself at the sill on a morning
whose seeds feel too tired to open, and decides
to take charge. "Let the affluent eastern sky
become the ghost of this whole machine
while an early-bird jogger churns past
adding foreground to those slow uphill curves
of the mesa road. And let the sun, rising, arrow
wildflowers back into the fields."

Like small memories from the belly of the mind
meadowlarks appear as he says, "Let no two of their gargles
quite repeat. Wherever I listen, let their shared theme
be variation." At a kitchen window with coffee
he says, "When the jogger returns on his downhill run
let him come casting, still, that cutter-bar shadow
fifty yards long, like Uncle Frank and the farm.
And let the sun, while I finish this cup, practice
trout scales on the power-plant reservoir."

"As for sparrows pecking blue seeds from shadows
behind Poston's fence, let them be blue themselves,
as long as I please. And let this sky I walk off
to work in manage an ultramarine so pure
that cactus along the path invent yellow keyholes
for bees. Let boughs of lodgepole pine compose
what the wind plays, in daylight prepared to believe
whatever I choose." Then steps out as if clear
on all that the morning had meant to be,
though, clearly, everything in it's amazed.

ANNA PRIMAVERA

Out of a cold and absolute wind which the tongue blurs on
it's spring, it's your name—Anne's self and voice—
when none of the fields hold still, none of their colors,
none of their birds, and least of all where blizzards
stacked up bone-heaviest alongside our fences.

From each thawed furrow how greenly
the phallic smoke rises! I decide to forget my drift
toward wherever, once the spine stiffens to the keel of a ship,
forget anything but this warmth I'd forgotten,
this woman whose turning to look
fits mine, and whose eyes and whose mouth, which isn't
and can't be less than annual miracle.

As if breath from stones? Something like that—
walking back and forth in simply your eyes
letting resinous weather from pine cones
give body to the forest, letting each skeletal rib and tibia
turn antenna for birdsong, letting my wintery tomb-lids lift
into blaze like cloud surprised to be burning alive
and freely as lately myself stepping into your smile
hands up and open, in the final praise of surrender.

THIS COULD HAVE BEEN THE PLACE

There is an angry, irritable desire we burn
as fuel, refusing to believe what we are
is anything like it. An invisible jet
chalklines west under June cirrus, its severe
functional aim relaxing slowly
with a general drift, an aimlessness
taking vapor curls one by one
for part of some intricate design.

Bursting at the seams all week
our big cottonwood lavishes an early cat
with millions of free balloons. Two insects
generating angular, whiskery legs couple
like a twin-rotor creature barely heavier
than air, floating off
on currents whose swarm and mix
confuses incredible cottonwood forests
with the ghosts of swallows.

I love these drapery folds that contour
our next-door hills—their metallic flashes
of jimson tip, bunch grass tassels
showing up sunburnt. And a week's
green rain still juicing
the rest of each stalk.

After such bad blood, such years
of irrelevant drive, I find myself
here. Standing quietly
a little past the center of a life
for which, who knows just how far back,
this could have been the place.

BONFIRES
for Jim Palmer

As the tossed match, catching, sets leaf nibbling leaf
we step back from the smashed melon smells of dead wood
into the layout of another's town sidewalks
and our first whiff of autumn on fire.
We think of this sky weighing tons
worn lightly as we play tag near the Illinois Braille
and Sight-Saving School, across wrought-iron fence
from a darkness born neutral and entire.

We think of our own school-mornings, dazzle on window scum
traversed by dawn's dead burdock, hairy clumps
lathering themselves in gold.

We think of the one face we still look for
distantly and far off as if in a candle flame
through the faces of others. Thinking of small ways
we ourselves will be missing,
we recall those farm-town afternoons raining on
and on like malicious copies of the soul.

But think too of catalpa—May leaves, May pods—
flocked cloverheads succulent as cornsilk; of August heat,
a torn knee shrugging flies away, of rust
fighting back where we crowbar nails
from a week's worth of second-hand lumber;
and of that twigless steppe crossing Kansas
into Colorado, a fast pickup miles and miles west
hauling-ass along gravelly side road, streaming slow
luminous billows of ochre.

We think of counting among irises opened on the face
of this ingenious earth, those eyelids now miming
an endless preference for stone; and of leafpiles
as all the words we have spoken to arrive at so little.
Thinking of ambitions recognizable only as strayed dogs
severed by train wheels, we consider how old
the wounds really are, and how much of our heaviness
may have been blood.

We think of snapped stalks fluttering;
pallid cornleaves fluttering under powerlines,
hedgerows of Osage orange where we overhear calls
answered by doves whose common color is dusk;
of quail flushed like a fist throwing up;
and of the high October hawks, idling,
then shearing the liquid air on wingspans
bursting, flaming.

With its leaves going up like a Cherokee bonnet
we think what daylight we've eaten, traveling,
and of these clarities incessantly given us
and of all we've been granted in secret, recalling
what red red bandanas we wore, once,
for keeping the wind awake years ago
where we are staring dead tired, content,
into the identical fire of this moment.

PART VII

SO THIS IS THE MAP

MOUNTAIN OF THE HOLY CROSS:
SAN JUAN RANGE

I

I rise through the holocaust of an old burn.

As if fire improving its past
each smatter of aspen leaf draws its pale green trunk
some 20, 30 feet up—the branches sassy
with a chitter and fluff of jays. Once, when it was still
a breathing universe, these aspen limbs trembled
that their wood had been nailed
to the death of a god.

Above, edge and jut. 10-acre pre-Cambrian thrust
taking wing on warps grotesque and plausible
as those continuous proofs of the insane.

II

Like hosts escaped from the pallid
fingers of priests, the sun haloes in flecks
of high cottonwood lint drifting east with root systems
in quest of themselves. Because the hardest places
to touch are those where nothing has died
or not nearly enough, I wish them valleys, and climb

toward the ice couloirs glittering like starlight
kindled in basalt, through wind-smells
musky with pools, through the billowing saxifrage—
aimless and deep as missing turns
of some maze. As if of this one
blueprinting each thumb.

III

How I love these shaken tussocks of vetch, eddies and flowings
of woodgrain blazed into relief by grit!
Its knurl on tamarisk root.
The quarter-sized sparkles of quartz pretending
to fit my hand like lost gifts. Here where reason
is all we have, and can never call us home
merely to dream of their power
seems to use it.

IV

Which is how we arrive
at the fabulous, out of an Illinois child who supposed
each mountaintop far to the west stood waiting
to tell him its story

turning out to be summit rock and a brain thinned
to this pillar of gnats
till its lung-beat catches up, letting me clear
and simplify with a view

whose only sound is scuffed air.

V

My parka hoodflap rackets one cheek with windburn
and sandpaper weather easing fracture lines
of whatever they knew. Miles below
through the systole, diastole of water vapor and heat
tempering the sky, tuning the distances for us
pine forest goes blue from eating blue dust
and stone sleep.
And the snowfields flash.

Within its nimbus of granite
broken somehow into tongues that make multitude
and solitude identical terms, my eye
is an immense detail
centering 360 degrees of haze peaks.

So this is the map.

Drifting in the still wheel of everything
giving rise to speech, I read it to say what we are
must always be where.

And my name's the edge of an intricate hole
the wind wants back, a pulse of burnt air,
a breath taken in, given up in this dream
that I came, and for no reason I know
was blessed by what cannot bless.

SCENE FOR AN EARLY
OCTOBER TO COME

for Wayne Dodd

Along toward sundown many forests
after this one, here
where trail dirt slumps off
onto shoreline, a hiker will slow
to a whisper.

Burnt meadows, red peaks. Brimming
lake puddled with gold; spatters of leaf
translucent as thin slices of lemon.
And evening sky lying down
between grass blades.

While shadows begin coming home
except for those of the clouds, now falling
far from the earth, that hiker will hesitate,
listening.

And yarrow will dither at his back
as glacial water sloshes and sighs like a well
turning itself inside out
all the way down into the valley.

Unable to say just who it is
he listens for; as if unknown to him
he once had a brother, here
where I'm standing.

ESSAY ON EARTH

I

Precisely. Pinching ourselves
what do we take between finger and thumb
if not their mixture of dust with time?
Otherwise, how could all of us
be standing here inside the question
and not be the key to it?

A short step. Magma buckles, cleaves open
like the wound in Adam's side. From its red chasm
a severed hand rises floating high
overhead, placing one luminous coin
in circulation
gazing down on the backroads
of vestiges, when light was still raw.

Moon as prolegomenal to what?

Perhaps to this voice
wearing its dark blue sky, kneeling now
beside the bed to say "Wake up,
you're dying."

II

From a Rock Island Line diner climbing
through drifts in mid-winter Sierras
it may be the snow Cadillac
whose dark windows, stuck on repeating "Home
sweet aardvark" have come along
ever since, allowing us to take in
Mommsen's stupendous 7-volume *History of Empire*
quick as a glass of dead ants.

III

Other times it may be odd as Hitler's watercolors,
all knife wine and cloud grease, but also
the jobless man lip reading want ads
for sacrifice enough to make sense—
or the aging Black whose only handle
is Texas John, never to make it
onto LP's or Library of Congress tapes
but still playing kinky upright piano that claims
his crippled left arm is where the blues go
when they've nowhere to go but in.

IV

Alone, it's an immigrant bohunk
listening his night lawn deep as an inlet
on the Baltic, where a forgotten rowboat—
both oars in place—knocks gently
against rocks too dark to see.

Simultaneously of course it could be
that Chinese pilgrim who borrowed
our only plough horse, dismounting now
at the pass, slapping rump
to start it back, a small gift
intricately strung to the harness.

V

It is those moments of deliverance
from this world's appearances
that deliver us into them. That salt flicker
when all our thresholds swerve, and we become
stadium sperm floating face down in fog,
or emptied pair of shoes
left neatly tied
just this side of the mirror.

90

VI

But isn't its clearest form that woman
we still hope to find
in whom the slightest improvement
would ruin everything? Never mind
that her notes, opened, prove
to be printed signatures, ours, saying
we were almost there.

Never mind. Even amongst those immortal few
generously including drunks, dead beats,
egomaniac pimps, isn't it Achilles' glory?
So full, so empty. Such ambitious pain,
and only the earth to cover it.

WHAT THE WIND SAYS

The wind says each
of these days has been mine.

But there is much
that still needs to be said.

Listen. The wind
has promised to say it.

NARCISSUS REFLECTS

Strolling out to ironize the scenery I leaned
on those whiffs of physics we called, once,
the wilderness of God. Dead wood? I seethed
animal invention into, out of each log,
took mountains along
lightly as burrs on my socks.

Masterful, my puppetry with trees! And those steam
butterflies, the clouds.

Drink it in and not reflect? How could I?

Hours pass in these waters
habitually mistaking, or years, who knows. Who knows
how it wastes me! Birds floating face down
in the air,
the sun stepping out of banked cumulus
like a woman stepping out of her clothes, these
that mirror the voice, its palimpsest glance—
endless, shadowy.

Because the eye hungers for more, the grotesque,
the mephitic, the scabrous. Starved for what's ugly!
And what do I see? Always the same splendor.

KNOWING ME WELL

Knowing me well you know
what evenings I've spent on ridgelines
toward sunset the light
the tuned palette
and clearly the distances
fading

to see how far
you could travel everywhichway
given time
and to possess it
only as light

seeping from creeks ravines
even cumulus

knowing me well you know
how I descend that mountain by dusk
thinking speed
of my shadow

because for a moment I stood
holding its arms out wide
as part of the rim
the planet's umbra extending

knowing me well you know
how going to sleep in the tent
I feel that shadow
continue

falling how far how far

and imagine what maybe just now
is swimming into its arms
and someday myself
passing through them

Born in downstate Illinois in 1931, REG SANER has mountaineered in Alaska and traveled in the Far East and Europe. As a Fulbright Scholar at the University of Florence, he studied Renaissance culture, and has since published translations of Italian and French writers. In 1976 Mr. Saner was awarded a creative-writing fellowship by the National Endowment for the Arts. He lives with his wife Anne and their two sons in Boulder, where he teaches at the University of Colorado.